Beginner's Guitar workout

Five minute of your day, ten times of your skill

Adam T Walls

Table of Content

chapter 1

Introduction

Learning to play the guitar is an exciting adventure that has the potential for both personal development and musical discovery. This carefully designed beginner's guitar exercise is meant to be your all-inclusive manual, providing a methodical route for those who are just starting out with six strings and melodies.

Adjusting the Musical Compass

Let's start with the fundamentals of guitar playing before delving into its complexities. The focus of Chapter 1 is tuning—that is, adjusting your instrument to produce melodies at the exact frequencies required. As you get more comfortable with the strings and develop your ear for pitch, the groundwork for the next musical journey will be laid.

The Sound's Anatomy

It's essential to comprehend a guitar's anatomy. Every component, ranging from the headstock to the body, adds to the resonance of the instrument. You will learn about the function of the frets, strings, and how your fingers are used in this chapter. Gaining confidence in your ability to travel the fretboard will enable you to unleash the possibilities for a variety of sounds.

Developing Dexterity in Fingers

You may find that learning to play the fretboard is a fun challenge: developing dexterity. Exercises to improve finger strength, flexibility, and accuracy are covered in Chapter 3. Smoother chord transitions and deft fingerpicking are made possible by these exercises, which are necessary for every budding guitarist.

Chords Revealed

The foundation of innumerable tunes are chords. We explore the realm of fundamental chords in this chapter, beginning with the fundamental open chords. Classics like C, G, and D will be taught to you, and you'll progressively add to your repertory. You'll enjoy making harmony as your fingers go over the frets and getting a kick out of knowing that chord pattern you know so well from your favorite songs.

Mastery of Rhythm

A trip with a guitar is never complete without learning rhythm. You'll learn about rhythmic approaches and strumming patterns in Chapter 5, which will help you bring your playing to life. You will get the rhythmic dexterity that separates a skilled guitarist from a beginner, starting with basic downstrokes and working your way up to complex strumming patterns.

Melodic Investigation

In Chapter 6, explore the world of melodies and single-note playing. You may enhance your guitar playing by adding a melodic element by learning to pluck single notes and simple tunes. These drills prepare you for lead roles and individual exploration in the future.

The Start of Your Musical Odyssey

As you go through this beginner's guitar exercise, keep in mind that learning a new instrument is a process rather than a final goal. Accept the difficulties, celebrate your successes, and follow the music's lead. This book

is your travel companion while you learn to play the guitar, whether your goal is to jam around a bonfire or take your skills to a stage. So turn up the volume, grab a melody, and start listening.Let's play some music.
The global language of music, which unites people and breaks down borders, extends an invitation for us to travel in harmony with one another. We enter a world where melody and rhythm meld to create a symphony of feelings when we get together to play some songs.

Picture a guitar being gently strung, the strings ringing out with each meaningful chord. The chamber fills with the warmth of the notes, beckoning listeners to experience the sensations of every strumming. The thrill of making music is unmatched, regardless of your level of experience; it's a great way to discover new sounds.

Our musical adventure is enhanced with a touch of elegance by the piano's magnificent keys. A waterfall of notes cascades over the ivory expanse while fingers dance, creating a tapestry of emotions. Every keystroke has a tale to tell, and we may piece it together by using the power of our common melodies.

Beats and rhythms are the main attraction for individuals who like the electronic genre. Our canvas is the skill of creating a smooth rhythm, adding layers to beats, and experimenting with soundscapes. Electronic music provides a dynamic arena for creativity, with everything from throbbing basslines to complex drum rhythms.

The human voice becomes an extremely potent means of expression when it is used outside of instruments. When our musical group performs heartfelt ballads or anthems, vocal harmonies give it a more personal touch. We weave a poetic tapestry of memories, dreams, and thoughts into the lyrics we sing, which captures the essence of our common experience.

In this group musical project, cooperation is essential. Everybody contributes their own voice, which adds to the overall harmony. We coordinate our efforts by practicing or improvising on the fly, resulting in a musical masterpiece that embodies the synthesis of several inspirations.

Remembering the audience, our silent traveling partners on this audio journey, is important. As artists, we get nourished by their responses, transforming the space into a dynamic, living organism. A symbiotic connection is formed between artists and audiences via the exchange of emotions, which enhances and deepens the musical experience.

Let the music lead the way as we get together to play some songs; it will transcend barriers and establish a deep connection between us. Let's compose a symphony that captures the spirit of our common humanity, whether it be with the expressive force of the human voice, the rhythmic pulse of electronic rhythms, or the traditional beauty of instruments. We'll create a tapestry of music together that will evoke feelings long after the last note fades.

  Acquiring the skill of holding a pick and playing in time signature
For every guitarist, knowing how to hold a pick and how to strumming in a certain time signature are essential abilities. Holding the pick firmly yet comfortably between your thumb and index finger is a good place to start. Try a variety of angles to see what seems most natural.

While strumming in a time signature, be aware of the rhythm pattern that corresponds to the selected meter, such as 3/4 or 4/4. Practice matching your hand movement to the rhythms while using steady downstrokes and upstrokes. As you develop confidence, progressively increase the pace while keeping a steady beat using a metronome.

Recall that accurate pick control and rhythmic strumming improve your guitar playing as a whole and provide a strong basis for more complex methods.

Chapter 2

Advance chords

Beyond the fundamental triads, advanced chords in music broaden the harmonic palette and give songs depth, intricacy, and color. These chords use longer notes and different tones to provide a more complex sound than the basic major and minor chords.

Seventh chords are a common kind of advanced chord. These chords are diminished seventh, dominant seventh, minor seventh, and major seventh. For example, the seventh note of the scale is introduced by the major seventh chord, which gives the tone a dreamy, luxurious character. On the other hand, the dominant seventh chord gives a feeling of energy and excitement by adding a tension that often resolves to thc tonic.

Extended chords provide even more intricacy by going beyond sevenths. By adding more tones, the ninth, eleventh, and thirteenth chords expand on the seventh chords. These chords are often used by performers that experiment with complex harmonies in the jazz and fusion genres. In addition to increasing the harmonic possibilities, the expanded chords provide distinctive voicings and soundscapes.

Furthermore, by changing certain notes in a chord, chromaticism is introduced. For example, the changed dominant chord adds tension and dissonance with its altered ninths and augmented or reduced fifths. These chords are common in musical genres that aim to defy conventional harmony, such as jazz and fusion.

An more sophisticated harmonic idea is modal exchange. It introduces surprising and captivating tonal alterations by appropriating chords from parallel scales. By briefly deviating from the main key, this method gives a piece more variation and intrigue.

Producers and composers of modern music often experiment with unconventional chord voicings and frameworks. While quartal and quintal harmony deviate from the more common thirds-based harmony by building chords based on intervals of fourths or fifths, cluster chords—where neighboring notes are played together—create a dense and discordant sound.

A strong foundation in music theory, ear training, and a great sense of musicality are necessary for using advanced chords. These chords are used by composers and musicians to express certain feelings, deepen arrangements, and experiment with traditional tonality.

To sum up, advanced chords provide a wide range of harmonic options in music. These complex harmonic ideas enhance the richness and complexity of musical works in a variety of genres, whether it is via the luscious sound of extended chords, the tension of changed chords, or the surprising turns of modal interchange. In the always changing field of music theory and practice, the territory of advanced chords continues to be a fascinating frontier for artists who are willing to experiment and develop.

Let's continue our chord study:

Examining chords in music is an intriguing way to learn about the harmonic underpinnings of many different kinds of songs. The foundation of musical harmony are chords, which are composed of three or more notes performed simultaneously. They add to the diverse range of sounds that enthrall listeners.

1. Major Chords: The major chord, which has a root note, major third, and perfect fifth, is one sort of fundamental chord. Major chords are widely used in upbeat and joyful musical sections, typically evoking sensations of brightness and solidity. Gaining an understanding of major chords lays a strong basis for understanding tonal connections in a composition.

2. Minor Chords: On the other hand, with a root note, minor third, and perfect fifth, minor chords bring in a distinct emotional character. In sharp contrast to the brightness of major chords, minor chords often evoke sentiments of sorrow or introspection. Understanding the subtle differences between major and minor chords improves one's capacity to express a range of emotions via music.

3. Seventh Chords: Adding to the exploration, seventh chords use the seventh note in addition to the root, third, and fifth, adding still another depth. These chords often add to the suspense and tension that characterize the jazz and blues genres. Comprehending seventh chords enhances the intricacy and profundity of an individual's understanding of harmonic structures.

4. Extended Chords: Musicians explore extended chords, which include ninth, eleventh, and thirteenth intervals, in addition to fundamental triads and seventh chords. These chords add to the harmonic palette's richness and complexity, giving improvisers and composers alike additional creative options.

5. Inversions and Voicings: Chord inversions and voicings are essential for boosting musical expression. While voicings describe the precise arrangement of the notes inside a chord, inversions require switching up the sequence in which the notes are played. Musicians may produce original and enthralling harmonic progressions by experimenting with voicings and inversions.

6. Practical Application: Mastery requires the application of academic knowledge to real-world situations. Musicians may absorb chord structures and get a greater comprehension of their acoustic influence by analyzing the chord progressions in their favorite songs or creating creative compositions.

In summary, the study of chords in music theory spans a wide and dynamic terrain. Chords in major, minor, seventh, and higher keys provide a range of feelings and options. The full potential of chords may be discovered by artists by study, application, and practice, which will allow them to express themselves musically to new heights.

Let's play some chords together.

Together, we will take a musical voyage into the fascinating realm of chords. The harmonic building blocks known as chords serve as the basis for a vast number of musical compositions. Playing chords is a basic and rewarding experience, regardless of your level of skill or desire to study.

Let us first clarify what a chord is. A chord is defined as a collection of three or more notes performed simultaneously in music theory. When these sounds are harmonized, they provide a rich, resonant sound that gives a composition depth and passion. Melodies are supported harmonically by chords, which give them a feeling of harmony and completion.

The major chord, which is distinguished by its upbeat and cheery tone, is one of the most often occurring chords. Place your fingers on the C, E, and G keys to play a chord in C major. When these notes are strung together, they create a melodic combination that perfectly captures the spirit of major chords.

Conversely, minor chords provide a tone that is more depressing and reflective. Change your finger position to cover C, E♭, and G for a C minor chord. Observe how the feeling subtly changes from major to minor, demonstrating the expressive power of chords in music.

Let's explore the realm of seventh chords now to add even more intricacy. For example, dominant seventh chords provide a sense of suspense and tension to the musical story. Try creating a G7 chord by mixing the notes G, B, D, and F. The seventh chords offer a dynamic interaction between suspense and conclusion.

When you experiment with chords, keep in mind inversions. A chord's voicing is changed when it is inverted, providing new insights and improving melodic coherence. Try out several chord inversions to find new tonal variations and soundscapes.

The power of chords cuts across genres and styles, whether you're utilizing a different instrument or strumming on a guitar or keyboard. In a wide range of musical genres, including pop, classical, jazz, and rock, chords serve as the common language that connects performers.

In summary, playing chords is a creative and expressive process as much as a test of technical proficiency. So pick up your instrument, surrender to the enchantment of harmony, and let the chords to lead you through the wide and alluring world of music.

Chapter 3

Warm-Up (5 minutes)

Any successful workout program must include warm-up activities because they help the body and mind get ready for higher intensity physical activity. These quick, focused sessions, which usually last five minutes or less, are essential for improving overall performance and lowering the risk of injury. A well-planned warm-up consists of a range of exercises that improve flexibility, target specific muscle groups, and raise heart rate gradually.

Increasing blood flow to the muscles, which provides them with the nutrition and oxygen they need for optimum performance, is one of the main objectives of a warm-up. This physiological reaction aids in increasing the body's core temperature, which loosens up and lessens the likelihood of strained or torn muscles. Cardiovascular activities that raise heart rate and improve blood circulation throughout the body, such mild jogging, jumping jacks, and skipping rope, are often included in warm-up regimens.

A successful warm-up should include dynamic stretching exercises in addition to aerobic exercises. In contrast to static stretching, which requires holding muscles still, dynamic stretching includes fluid, controlled motions that allow joints to fully extend. Stretching of this kind enhances joint mobility, flexibility, and coordination, all of which lead to improved performance in later activities. Arm circles, torso twists, and leg swings are a few types of dynamic stretches.

A comprehensive warm-up also targets the particular muscle groups that will be used during the main activity. This might include working those regions with mild, bodyweight workouts. For example, bodyweight lunges or squats might be included in the warm-up if the activity is primarily focused on the lower body. The muscles are engaged and activated during these exercises, readying them for heavier weights and actions later in the workout.

Warm-ups provide psychological advantages in addition to physical ones. They provide a transitional phase during which people may turn their attention from their regular activities to the impending exercise. This mental preparation may improve focus and foster an optimistic outlook, which will eventually raise the caliber of the workout. Warming up may also be seen as a ritual that heralds the start of a focused and intentional training session.

In conclusion, the efficiency and safety of an exercise may be greatly impacted by spending as little as five minutes on a well-planned warm-up. Through enhanced blood flow, enhanced flexibility, and mental readiness for physical activity, people lower their risk of injury and position themselves for best performance. Warm-up activities should be seen as an essential component of a whole fitness program that helps achieve long-term health and fitness objectives, rather than just a formality.

Finger stretches for a beginner's guitar workout:

It's a gratifying experience to play the guitar, but it requires dexterity and finger flexibility. It is essential, particularly for beginners, to include finger stretches in your practice regimen to improve your playing and avoid pain or damage.

1. Finger Spread: Start by laying your hand flat with your fingers together on a surface. Stretch your fingers apart as far as you can and maintain the position for ten to fifteen seconds. To increase the independence and agility of your fingers, repeat this several times.

2. Individual Finger Stretches: Maintain the other fingers up and isolate each finger by pushing it against a flat surface. After a brief period of holding, go on to the next finger. This workout improves control and strength in your fingers.

3. Finger Tapping: Make sure every finger receives equal attention by lightly tapping it on a table or other hard surface. This practice enhances coordination and finger awareness, both of which are necessary for playing complex guitar chords.

4. Thumb Stretch: Press your thumb gently on the base of your pinky finger to extend it. Hold, let go, and repeat

after a little while. This stretch focuses on the range of motion of the thumb, which is important for chord changes.

5. Reverse Finger Stretch: Hold your hand with the fingers outstretched and the palm pointing downward. Using your other hand, gently draw each finger back towards the wrist. This stretch improves finger flexibility by focusing on the undersides of the fingers.

6. Spider Walk: Start on a level surface, then raise and lower each finger individually to make a crawling motion. This is a great workout to build finger strength, control, and independence since it mimics the movement needed to play chords on a guitar.

7. Wrist Flexibility: To keep your hands as flexible as possible, rotate them both clockwise and counterclockwise. In order to avoid stiffness and encourage fluidity in your playing, this stretch is essential.

8. Finger Rolls: Roll each finger separately and collectively in a circular motion. This exercise increases finger mobility generally, improves blood circulation, and lessens stiffness.

Include these stretches for your fingers in your regular guitar practice regimen. Set aside some time to warm up your hands before you play. Maintaining consistency is essential. Gradually, you'll feel an improvement in finger strength, agility, and accuracy, which will set the stage for more competent and pleasurable guitar playing.

Exercises for strumming:

Learning how to strumming is essential to become a proficient string player, especially on the guitar. The goal of these drills is to improve the player's general instrument control, rhythm, and strumming technique. Whether you're a novice or an accomplished musician, practicing strumming exercises regularly will greatly improve your abilities.

1. Fundamental Strumming Techniques:
To build a solid foundation, start with basic upstrokes and downstrokes. Work on different combinations, such down-up-down-up, to improve your strumming hand's coordination and fluency.

2. Rhythmic Variations: To hone your sense of time, play around with various rhythmic patterns. Your playing will have more dynamics and become more captivating if you use syncopated strumming and emphasize particular rhythms.

3. Dynamic Control: Pay attention to changing how hard you strumming. For a more dramatic impact, try strumming more forcefully after practicing quietly for a more soothing tone. Your playing gains more expressiveness with this dynamic control.

4. Chord Progressions: Mix standard chord progressions with strumming drills. This improves your ability to strum in time with various musical situations as well as aids in grasping chord changes.

5. Palm Muting: Include methods for palm muting in your strumming drills. To create a muted, percussive sound, softly place the edge of your hand on the strings close to the bridge. Gaining proficiency in this method is necessary for playing a variety of genres, but particularly blues and rock.

6. Genre-Specific Strumming Patterns:
Make your strumming drills more appropriate for certain genres, such as jazz, reggae, or folk. You may adjust to a variety of musical genres by learning the distinctive strumming patterns of each genre.

7. Pick vs. Fingerstyle Strumming: Try both pick and fingerstyle strumming techniques. Every approach has a unique tone and may be used with a variety of musical styles. Gaining expertise in both methods increases your guitarist's flexibility.

**8. ** Accuracy and Velocity: Gradually raise the tempo of your strumming while retaining accuracy. Accurate and quick strumming is essential for performing complex sections and will help you become a better player overall.

Syncing with Drum Beats: Get comfortable strumming in time with either drum beats or a metronome. This keeps your strumming in time with the rhythm section in a band context and aids in the development of a good sense of timing.

10. Originality and Improvisation: After you've gotten the hang of things, try incorporating some originality into your strumming. Try different rhythms, add pauses, and improvise to create a distinctive sound that expresses your individuality as a musician.

To sum up, practicing strumming exercises consistently and intently is essential to developing into a skilled guitarist. These exercises help you become more technically proficient while also improving your general musicality, which will help you communicate with your instrument more effectively.

chord Progressions (15 minutes)

The fundamental building blocks of music are chord progressions, which give songs their harmonic foundation and determine the piece's overall emotional tone. They are chord progressions performed in a certain order that make up a song's harmonic framework. For musicians, composers, and songwriters, knowing chord progressions is crucial since they foster creativity and add to the overall attractiveness of a piece of music.

A typical chord progression seen in many genres, including pop, rock, and blues, is I-IV-V. For example, this progression uses the chords C, F, and G in the key of C major. The scale degrees of the chords in the key are indicated by the Roman numerals. Numerous popular songs are built around this simple but effective development.

The ii-V-I progression, which is often used in jazz music, is another notable progression. It contains the chords Dm7, G7, and Cmaj7 in the key of C major. This progression demonstrates the adaptability of chord progressions in a variety of genres by producing a sleek and elegant sound.

Certain emotions may be evoked by chord progressions. A major key progression, such as I-V-vi-IV, often expresses a more upbeat and hopeful vibe, but a minor key progression, such as i-iv-VII, may produce a sad ambiance. Musicians may customize the emotional effect of their works by experimenting with various progressions.

A useful tool for comprehending and constructing chord progressions is the Circle of Fifths. It makes it simpler to find matching chords by arranging keys according to their connections. Investigating the relationships between the keys in the Circle of Fifths creates new avenues for the creation of captivating and lively progressions.

Another factor in the development of chord progressions has been technology. Musicians may experiment with chord progressions digitally utilizing digital audio workstations (DAWs) and software synthesizers, which speeds up the creative process. AI programs may also find recurrent progressions in well-known songs, which might inspire artists.

To sum up, chord progressions are an essential part of the musical language. Composing distinctive and emotionally charged pieces requires an awareness of and willingness to experiment with chord progressions, whether you're generating electronic music, playing the piano, or strumming a guitar. These fundamental musical elements—from the straightforward I-IV-V to the intricate jazz progressions—continue to influence the wide range of musical expression.

Typical open chords

Typical Open Chords: The Basis for Guitar Performance

Open chords are the foundation of many guitar songs in a variety of genres and are essential to learning how to play the instrument. The reason these chords are referred to as "open" is because they have open strings, which give your playing more depth and richness. We'll go over some of the most popular open chords here that every guitarist needs to know how to play.

Major C (C):

Place your fingers on the D, A, and B strings' second fret. The remaining ones are left open-ended.
Bright and adaptable, this chord is often used in folk and pop music.
G Major:

Put your fingers on the low E string's third fret and the second fret of the A string, leaving the other frets free.
A common and strong chord used in many different genres, including country and rock.
D Major: D

Put your fingers on the G string's second fret and the B string's third fret. Keep the other strings untied.
A common chord in folk and acoustic music, it is warm and resonant.

25

Major A (A):

formed by putting your fingers on the D, G, and B
strings' second frets.
a flexible chord often heard in pop and rock music.
Major E (E):

Put your fingers on the G string's first fret, the A string's
second fret, and the high E string's first fret. Play the
remaining portions unplugged.
a standard chord with a strong, brilliant tone that may be
found in many genres.
D Minor (Dm):

Lift the index finger to make the high E string sound
open, just as in the D Major.
a depressing chord that's often used in ballads and
slower pieces.
A Minor (Am):

Play by depressing the B string's first fret. Play the other
strings open.
a common and adaptable chord, particularly in classical
and acoustic music.
E Minor (Em):

formed by putting your fingers on the A and D strings'
second frets.
a chord that is used in many different musical genres
that has a somewhat melancholy tone.

Gaining proficiency in these popular open chords can provide a strong basis for your guitar learning. As you advance, you'll learn how to mix and alter these chords to produce countless melodic combinations. These open chords are a guitarist's best friend, whether you're experimenting with your own compositions or just strumming along to your favorite tunes. You may use these fundamental components to their fullest extent in your musical undertakings if you continue to practice and experiment.

Chord transitions: When playing an instrument, especially a strung one like a guitar or ukulele, chord transitions are essential. For music to sound unified and pleasurable, chord changes must be learned and executed with accuracy.

The ability to transition between chords with ease is essential for preserving harmony and rhythm. Chord changes may be difficult for beginners at first, but with repetition, muscle memory builds and the process becomes more natural.

Hand placement is a crucial component of effective chord changes. To enable fast and accurate adjustments, each finger must effectively locate its home on the fretboard. In addition to ensuring a good sound, placing your fingers correctly shortens the time between chords.

Timing is also another important factor. A well-timed transition improves a musical piece's overall flow. By using a metronome during practice, musicians may better absorb the beat and achieve more seamless and coordinated chord changes.

Many compositions are constructed using common chord progressions, therefore learning how to handle transitions within these progressions is an important ability. Across many genres, progressions like C-G-Am-F or E-A-D-B are common and provide a great starting point for learning chord changes.

Moreover, varying the strumming patterns and picking styles throughout transitions gives the song greater depth and energy. Chord changes may be made more captivating and fascinating by experimenting with different strumming or fingerpicking techniques.

Smooth chord transitions are influenced by mental preparation in addition to technical factors. A musician may become more proficient at changing chords quickly by visualizing the chord forms that will be played and by anticipating the next step. This mental rehearsal enhances physical rehearsal and advances total skill.

In order to accelerate their learning process, musicians often identify difficult transitions and rehearse them again. Increasing speed gradually as accuracy rises is a tried-and-true way to develop dexterity and confidence.

Lastly, there is still work to be done in order to perfect chord transitions. All levels of musicians always work to improve their skills and broaden their repertory by experimenting with different chord progressions. Whether performing simple folk songs or intricate jazz pieces, the ability to smoothly switch between chords is a dynamic talent that develops with every musical project.

Chapter 5

Finger style Techniques (10 minutes)
With fingerstyle guitar skills, players may produce complex, rich sounds using their fingers instead of a pick, showcasing a varied and expressive approach to playing. Many genres, including folk, blues, classical, and even current pop, use this method often. Let's examine some important fingerstyle technique elements during the following ten minutes.

1. Correct Hand Method:

Fingerstyle: This technique uses the thumb, index, middle, and ring fingers to pluck various strings, each producing a distinct tone.
Alternating Bass: To establish a rhythmic basis, a basic approach is to alternate the bass notes between the thumb and other fingers.
2. Patterns of Fingerpicking:

Merle Travis inspired the name "Travis Picking," a well-known pattern that consists of a constant alternating bass line and melody notes played with the other fingers.
Clawhammer Method: This method, which is popular in folk and bluegrass music, produces a unique percussion sound by using the nails to play downward.
3. Harmonious Melody Method:

Simultaneous Chords and Melody: Fingerstyle guitar enables players to combine melody and chords in a fluid way, resulting in a full arrangement on a single instrument.
4. Tapping and Harmonics:

Natural Harmonics: Ethereal tones may be added to the song by gently stroking certain locations on the strings to form harmonics.
Tapping: This method, which was adapted from electric guitar playing, includes tapping the fretboard with the right hand's fingers to produce a wider range of tones.
5. Exercises for Thumb Independence:

Isolating Thumb Movements: In order to perform complex patterns, it is essential to develop separate thumb control. Exercises using only your thumbs may assist develop this ability.
6. Static Management:

Accenting and Ghost Notes: By focusing on certain notes or adding subtly omitted ghost notes, fingerstyle enhances expressiveness and allows for delicate dynamics.
Fingerstyle in Various Genres: **7.**

Classical Fingerstyle: Distinguished by its complex compositions and methodical approach.
Fingerstyles of folk and blues music emphasize improvisation and rhythmic patterns.

Modern Fingerstyle: Experiments with cutting-edge methods, often fusing several genres to create a fresh sound.
8. Mastery of Fingerstyle:

Chet Atkins: Highly regarded for his contributions to country music and thumbstyle technique.
Tommy Emmanuel: Well-known for his breathtaking fingerstyle acts.
The evolution of fingerstyle technique was inspired by the work of classical guitarist Andres Segovia.
**9. ** Useful Advice for Fingerstyle Performers:

Upkeep of the Nails: To get the proper tone, fingerstyle players must keep their right-hand nails in good condition.
Relaxed Technique: Improving dexterity and quickness requires releasing tension from the hands and fingers.
10. New Developments in Fingerstyle:

Extended Techniques: Contemporary fingerstyle musicians are always pushing the envelope by experimenting with percussion components, different tunings, and unorthodox methods.
In summary, fingerstyle approaches provide guitarists with an immense and fascinating array of options. Discovering the subtleties of fingerstyle may open up new avenues for creative expression and musical inventiveness, regardless of skill level. Spend some time learning, honing, and customizing these six-string methods.

Identifying patterns with your fingers:

Guitarists use fingerpicking patterns as a flexible and expressive method to construct complex and melodic combinations. Using the fingers, each guitar string is individually plucked to create a rich, complex sound that is distinct from strumming. There are many patterns, each giving the song a unique quality.

The Travis Picking technique is among the most basic fingerpicking patterns. This pattern, which takes its name from country musician Merle Travis, alternates between bass and melody and harmony notes. It's popular throughout genres since it offers a basis for rhythm while allowing for the insertion of complex melodies.

The Classical Fingerstyle, which is popular in both classical and flamenco music, is another often used pattern. This method, which uses all fingers to articulate various strings, stresses control and accuracy. The guitarist's technical skill is shown via the use of sophisticated arrangements and dramatic emotion that come with the classical fingerstyle.

The Piedmont Fingerpicking technique is quite popular in folk and blues music. This style, which is typified by a syncopated and alternating bassline, often uses a thumbpick to increase speed and clarity. Fingerpicking artists like as Elizabeth Cotten and Mississippi John Hurt are highly regarded for their proficiency on this technique.

Folk and bluegrass musicians often use the Clawhammer Fingerstyle, which is characterized by a downward strumming action with the fingernail or picks that mimics a clawhammer. This percussive and rhythmic approach, which originated with the banjo, has permeated guitar playing as well, giving acoustic compositions a distinctive touch.
Fingerstyle patterns provide guitarists a lot of creative space to express their own musical voices. By experimenting with various patterns and approaches, musicians enhance the realm of acoustic guitar music and add to the progress and variety of fingerpicking genres. Fingerpicking patterns continue to be a fascinating and vital part of the guitarist's toolbox, whether they are reminiscent of the blues, classical music, or the narrative quality of folk music.

cooperation between the thumb and fingers:

One of the most important aspects of fine motor abilities is thumb and finger coordination, which is essential for many everyday tasks. Humans are able to execute tasks with accuracy, dexterity, and control because of the complex dance between the thumb and fingers.

Thumb and Finger Anatomy: The thumb and fingers are essential parts of the human hand, which is a wonder of biomechanical ingenuity. Among primates, humans are the only ones with an opposable thumb, which allows for a variety of grips and motions. With their joints and muscles, the fingers and thumb cooperate to create an intricate coordination system.

Development in Infancy: As infants investigate their environment, the development of thumb and finger coordination starts. These abilities are honed by grasping items, which lays the groundwork for subsequently complex motions. Simple activities like gripping a caregiver's finger or holding a bottle increasingly become more difficult.

Fine Motor Skills: Children's ability to coordinate their thumbs and fingers becomes more refined as they develop. Fine motor abilities are developed via tasks like buttoning clothing, tying shoelaces, and handling tiny things. The need of these coordination abilities in early school is shown by the fact that they are essential for academic assignments like writing and drawing.

Essential for Daily Tasks: We use our thumb and finger coordination all the time. The capacity to control items with precision is a testimony to the complex coordination between the thumb and fingers. Examples of this coordination include typing on keyboards and utilizing cellphones, as well as cooking, crafts, and performing musical instruments.

Sports and Hobbies: Thumb and finger coordination is crucial in sports, especially those that require hand-eye coordination, like basketball or playing an instrument like the piano. To perform at their best, artists and athletes alike depend on the exact movement of their fingers.

Rehabilitation and Therapy: Specific exercises are commonly used in rehabilitation to improve the coordination of the thumb and fingers in those who have had hand injuries or disorders that impair motor abilities. Various strategies are used by occupational therapists to enhance hand strength, flexibility, and general functioning.

Aging and Difficulties: It's crucial to maintain ideal thumb and finger coordination as people age. These skills may be impacted by conditions such as arthritis, which calls for the use of adaptive methods and treatments in order to minimize difficulties and preserve independence.

To sum up, thumb and finger coordination are complex abilities that affect many facets of our life. Our general usefulness and well-being are greatly enhanced by our ability to coordinate these digits, from early childhood development to the limitations of age. Maintaining an active and healthy lifestyle requires an understanding of and development of this synergy.

Chapter 6

Melody and Riffs (10 minutes)

With the use of a wide range of methods, fingerstyle guitarists may produce complex and expressive music with only their fingertips. This adaptable technique adds a subtle and intimate touch to the instrument by using individual fingers to pluck or strumming the notes.

The employment of the thumb, index, middle, and ring fingers—each corresponding to a different string—is a basic component of fingerstyle. This enables simultaneous harmony, bass lines, and melody—a feature that characterizes the intricacy of fingerstyle. A traditional method of playing fingerstyle guitar is to use the fingers for melody and the thumb for bottom notes, creating a polyphonic texture that sets fingerstyle apart from other guitar playing genres.

In order to create varied tonal characteristics, fingerstyle musicians often use a variety of right-hand approaches. The "rest stroke" produces a warm, resonant tone by plucking a string and then resting the finger on the string next to it. On the other hand, by allowing the finger to wander away from the strings after plucking, the "free stroke" produces a brighter tone.

Players use hammer-ons, pull-offs, and slides in addition to normal fingerpicking to increase expressiveness. These additions give the song more vibrancy and color, making for an engrossing listen. Fingerstyle players may expand their range of tones by adding percussion components such as tapping or slapping the guitar body.

Players may also combine chords, arpeggios, and single-note lines with ease while using fingerstyle. The elaborate arrangements that emerge from this blending of methods highlight the guitar's wide spectrum of possibilities. Fingerstyle musicians use their finger patterns, dynamics, and stylistic details to create a distinct voice, whether they are covering well-known songs or creating original works.

Furthermore, fingerstyle methods differ in many genres, including folk, blues, classical, and even modern. Fingerstyle has been pioneered and popularized by musicians like as Chet Atkins, Tommy Emmanuel, and Andy McKee in a variety of musical contexts, demonstrating its versatility and ageless appeal.

Fingerstyle demands accuracy and patience since it's important to learn each individual finger movement. Establishing a consistent rhythm and fostering finger independence are fundamental abilities that prepare the way for more complex methods. The development and adaptability of a musician are facilitated by consistent practice and exposure to a variety of fingerstyle arrangements.

To sum up, fingerstyle methods provide an engaging way to play the guitar and let players experiment with a wide variety of melodic options. Fingerstyle continues to be a timeless and expressive technique that enthralls and inspires players and listeners alike, whether it is used to the subtle subtleties of classical works or the rhythmic intricacy of modern arrangements.

Simple tunes:

Basic melodies provide a recognized and memorable note sequence that forms the basis of musical creations. From classical to current music, these foundational melodic phrases are vital in a variety of musical styles. A melody is usually composed of a rhythmically ordered series of pitches that are placed in a linear fashion to produce a coherent and emotive musical message.

The most basic melodies often have a simple contour, progressing stepwise or with little gaps between notes. This simplicity helps to produce hummable, easily remembered melodies. As their knowledge of music theory grows, artists may experiment with more intricate melodic structures that include syncopation, leaps, and a variety of rhythmic rhythms.

Scales are groupings of pitches grouped in either ascending or descending order that are used to create melodies. Common scales, including the major and minor scales, provide the fundamentals for composing melodies that are both visually beautiful and harmonically rich. A melody's emotional quality may be influenced by the scale used; major scales suggest a brighter, lighter feel, whereas minor scales suggest a more dramatic or melancholy tone.

A fundamental component in creating simple melodies is repetition. Repeated phrases or motifs are often used by musicians to build rapport and a feeling of coherence throughout a piece. Variations on a melodic theme may also provide complexity and intrigue, which keeps listeners interested throughout the whole musical experience.

Although fundamental melodies are essential to musical structure, a whole musical experience is created by their interaction with other components including harmony, rhythm, and dynamics. A composition's depth and richness are increased by harmony, which is produced by combining many melodies or by using chords as accompaniment. The time and tempo of melodic phrases are governed by rhythm, which also affects the general feel and groove of the song.

One of the most important things to learn in the field of composing is how to write simple songs. Composers and musicians utilize melodies to attract audiences, tell tales, and transmit emotions, whether via meticulous design or improvisation. Basic melodies continue to be a timeless and universal component in the enormous tapestry of musical expression, from the catchy tunes of pop songs to the complex lines of classical pieces.

First riffs:

A song's opening riffs establish the mood and capture the attention of the audience. They are its beating heart. These little melodic lines, which are meant to stick in the mind, act as a musical greeting card, bringing the listener into the composition's auditory realm. Introductory riffs are the initial paint stroke on the canvas of a musical journey, from memorable keyboard melodies to guitar riffs that define whole genres. Opening Riffs: Uncovering Musical Doors

Within the broad world of music, opening riffs serve as the friendly gatekeepers to auditory experiences. These succinct yet impactful melodic lines play a vital part in defining a song's personality. Think of the signature guitar lines from Metallica's "Enter Sandman" or the famous opening riff from Led Zeppelin's "Whole Lotta Love"; these initial riffs are the melodic handshakes that entice the listener into a realm of musical narrative.

Introductory riffs are similar to literary prologues in that they provide a preview of the main ideas that will be covered. These are the tonal characteristics that define a composition's emotional climate, genre, and mood. Every genre has a repertoire of opening riffs that are designed to fascinate and mesmerize, from the heartfelt wails of a saxophone in jazz to the thrilling crunch of distorted guitars in rock and metal.

Particularly guitar riffs have come to be associated with rock music and all of its subgenres. The bluesy swagger of Chuck Berry's "Johnny B. Goode" or the chugging power chords of AC/DC's "Back in Black" are ingrained in popular culture. These opening themes not only establish the songs but also often go beyond them to become icons of popular culture.

However, opening riffs don't have to be played on the guitar's six strings. At the start of a song, keyboards, basslines, and even vocal melodies may make their mark and invite the listener to embark on an unforgettable auditory adventure. Think of the catchy bassline that opens Queen's "Another One Bites the Dust" or the eerie piano intro of Pink Floyd's "Shine On You Crazy Diamond" as examples of the variety and inventiveness that can be found in opening riffs.

These riffs are more than just notes on a sheet of music; they are emotive. They create the emotional tone for the events that follow and might be thrilling, depressing, suspenseful, or victorious. A storyteller in and of itself, the opening riff teases the listener to go further into the musical tale by giving a preview of what's to come.

To sum up, opening riffs serve as the sparkplugs for musical discovery. They have the power to arouse feelings of longing, excitement, and anticipation. The beginning notes of a musical conversation that entices us to listen, feel, and experience the wonder of sound are introduction riffs, which may be the twang of a country guitar, the syncopated rhythms of a hip-hop track, or the classical beauty of a piano.

Chapter 7

Rhythm and Timing (10 minutes)
In dance, music, and many other creative mediums, rhythm and timing are essential components. They act as the framework, directing the composition's or performance's flow and structure. For both artists and viewers, the complex interaction between rhythm and time produces a dynamic and captivating experience.

The structured arrangement of sounds and silences in music, often conveyed by a steady beat, is known as rhythm. On the other hand, timing entails the exact application of these rhythmic components in a designated area. Together, they set the tempo and mood of a piece of music, affecting the emotional resonance of the work.

Think of a drumbeat as the basic rhythmic pulse of many different musical styles. The rhythm's consistency or syncopation is largely dependent on the time of each drum stroke. Electronic music may use exact, machine-like time for a particular sound, whereas jazz, for example, relies on complex timing fluctuations.

Timing and rhythm take on a bodily aspect in dancing. Dancers create a mesmerizing blend of sound and motion as they time their moves to musical pulses. In dance, timing is crucial to expressiveness because it allows artists to tell stories and portray emotions with perfectly timed jumps, spins, and gestures.

Timing and rhythm are essential in everyday life even outside of the arts. For instance, speech employs syllable and pause rhythms to create cadences that facilitate communication. Athletes time their motions perfectly to attain peak performance in sports, whether it's a sprinter breaking out of the starting blocks or a basketball player making a perfectly timed pass.

Timing and rhythm are important in many areas, including neurology and technology. Digital audio workstations used in music creation depend on exact time to smoothly organize and synchronize many songs. Research in neuroscience reveals links between rhythm processing and cognitive capacities by examining the ways in which rhythm affects brain function.

In summary, time and rhythm are omnipresent factors that influence how we perceive dance, music, communication, and everyday activities. In our varied and linked environment, their subtle interactions offer depth and variety to the fabric of human expression, highlighting how important it is to comprehend and value these fundamental components.

Metronome exercises:

One of the most important and useful tools for improving one's musical abilities is metronome practice. The metronome is a vital instrument for every musician, regardless of skill level, since it helps you to acquire and sustain time, rhythm, and accuracy in your performance.

First and foremost, the metronome serves as a dependable guide for artists of all genres by providing a steady and regular beat. This steady pulse facilitates the learning of intricate rhythms, enhances overall musicianship, and improves synchronization between various instruments. It fosters a tighter and more coherent sound by establishing discipline and assisting players in keeping pace with the piece.

Internal timing development is one of the main advantages of metronome practice. Musicians who use a metronome for practice on a daily basis are better able to keep a constant pace on their own. When it comes to live performances, teamwork, and recording sessions when accuracy is critical, this internalized sense of time is essential.

Practice using a metronome is especially helpful for musicians who are learning new compositions or honing ones they already know. In order to ensure correctness and fluency, musicians might methodically practice on challenging parts by beginning at a modest pace and progressively increasing speed. This gradual method not only helps students learn well, but it also prevents undesirable habits from forming from trying to play too quickly or too quickly.

The metronome not only helps with pace control but also with dynamic expressiveness. Within the parameters of a steady rhythm, musicians may play around with different articulations, accents, and phrasing. This simultaneous emphasis on emotion and accuracy results in a musical performance that is complex and well-rounded.

The metronome unites the time of many musicians in an ensemble performance by acting as a unifying factor. This is particularly important in collaborative settings like orchestras and bands, where synchronization is essential to producing a polished and well-rounded sound.

To sum up, metronome practice is a vital skill for musicians of all skill levels. It develops musical discipline and raises the quality of the performance overall by honing time, rhythm, and accuracy. Musicians may improve and reach new heights of skill by making metronome practice a regular part of their regimen.

Variations in strumming:

You may include distinctive rhythmic patterns and tones into your song by using different strumming patterns, which give your guitar playing more depth and dramatic flare. Developing a variety of strumming approaches is essential to producing interesting and varied musical works.

Changing the strum's direction and strength is one popular strumming variation. Try alternating upstrokes and downstrokes to create a rhythmic contrast. You may achieve subtle tones in your playing, ranging from delicate fingerpicking to forceful full-chord strums, by adjusting the strength of your strumming hand.

Another useful strumming technique that adds odd accents to your performance is syncopation. Your song may gain intensity and depth by highlighting unexpected rhythms. To create the illusion of syncopation, divide beats into smaller segments and add pauses.

Try out other strumming patterns, such the well-known "swing" rhythm, which gives your playing a shuffling, groove-focused vibe. To provide a feeling of unpredictability and to keep listeners interested, use a variety of strumming patterns throughout the song.

By adding hand muting to your strumming repertoire, you may change the guitar's tone and produce a percussion-like sound. Play around with where and how hard you put your hand on the strings to get the right amount of mute resonance and clarity.

Slides, pull-offs, and hammer-ons are examples of embellishments that may be used to improve strumming variants. Use these methods to include melodic aspects into your strumming patterns and reach new levels in your guitar playing.

Ultimately, practice and perseverance are needed to become proficient with strumming variants. Try out various combinations of approaches and see how they affect the music's overall vibe. Strumming variants are a flexible tool to express your musical inventiveness, whether you're performing electric rock, folk acoustic, or any other genre.

Chapter 8

Cool Down (5 minutes)

Any workout program must include cooling down. This step is often missed but is critical for enhancing general health and avoiding injury. Usually lasting five minutes or so, the main goal of the cool-down phase is to gradually return the body to its pre-exercise condition.

A variety of activities may be included in this short time to facilitate the shift from vigorous physical activity to rest. Low-intensity aerobic activity, such brisk walking or mild cycling, is one strategy that is often used. By maintaining blood circulation and progressively lowering heart rate, these exercises facilitate the elimination of metabolic waste products that are produced during physical activity.

Another essential component of a thorough cool-down is static stretching. Stretches should be held for 15 to 30 seconds, concentrating on the main muscle groups engaged throughout the exercise. This will increase muscular tension and promote flexibility. In the long run, this may help to increase range of motion and lessen the chance of pain after exercise.

Apart from its physical advantages, the cool-down facilitates a mental shift. The body transitions from an elevated state of awareness to a more relaxed one when the pulse rate drops and breathing resumes its regular rhythm. This kind of mental adjustment may help lower stress and increase wellbeing.

Crucially, a well performed cool-down may help avoid injuries. Muscle stiffness and an elevated risk of injury may result from abruptly ceasing vigorous activity without allowing the body to progressively restore to its baseline condition. A healthy cool-down may protect people's bodies and improve their entire exercise experience in as little as five minutes.

In conclusion, even though the cool-down stage of an exercise session could seem to be a brief and unimportant component, its advantages are extensive. Including a deliberate 5-minute cool-down in your workout regimen increases flexibility, decreases discomfort in your muscles, and promotes mental clarity in addition to helping you avoid injuries. It's an inexpensive yet effective investment on your quest toward total health and fitness.

Soft stretches:

Stretching gently is essential for preserving flexibility, easing stress in the muscles, and enhancing general wellbeing. The focus of these workouts is comfort over intensity, with slow, deliberate movements. There are many advantages for your body and mind when you include mild stretches into your everyday practice.

A major benefit of doing mild stretches is that they increase flexibility. Our muscles tend to become tighter as we get older or live sedentary lives, which reduces our flexibility. By lengthening muscles and expanding their range of motion, mild stretching on a regular basis helps offset this. Improved flexibility helps with everyday tasks by improving posture, lowering the chance of injury, and making movement easier.

Additionally, mild stretches aid in stress reduction and relaxation. These exercises help people release tension from different muscle groups and concentrate on their breathing since they are slow and methodical. This has a beneficial effect on mental health in addition to reducing physical stress. A daily practice that includes mild stretches may promote balance and peace by acting as a relaxing ritual.

Apart from the psychological and physical advantages, mild stretches may be modified to suit different levels of fitness and medical concerns. These stretches are adaptable to your requirements, regardless of your experience level or if you're recuperating from an ailment. In order to prevent strain or damage, it's important to pay attention to your body and move within a comfortable range.

Think about arranging short, easy stretches throughout the day. Your body may be gently stretched as part of your morning ritual to help wake it up and get ready for the day. Stretching during the midday may help improve circulation and lessen stiffness while offering a much-needed respite from work or other sedentary pursuits. Stretching in the evening may be especially helpful in releasing tension that has accumulated during the day, which can help you get a better night's sleep.

Finally, mild stretches provide a comprehensive strategy for preserving both physical and mental health. These exercises are a great way to add some flexibility, relaxation, and adaptation to anyone's everyday routine. Embracing moderate stretches may be a worthwhile investment in your self-care journey, whether your goal is to improve your general health or just find some quiet time.

Play that is reflective:

Through a variety of play activities, reflective play is a stimulating and energizing activity that allows people—especially kids—to examine their ideas, feelings, and experiences. Reflective play, in contrast to typical play, places a strong emphasis on self-awareness, introspection, and cognitive involvement. This method improves social and emotional intelligence in addition to aiding in personal growth.

People participate in activities that challenge them to reflect critically on their emotions and behaviors when they play reflectively. Role-playing, storytelling, or even easy games that promote emotional expression and reflection may be used to do this. In this way, reflective play turns into an effective instrument for understanding and self-discovery.

The capacity of reflective play to promote empathy is one of its main features. By means of creative situations and role-playing, individuals adopt diverse viewpoints, acquiring comprehension of the emotions and encounters of others. This fosters compassion and a greater comprehension of emotions, two qualities that are necessary for positive social relationships.

Because reflective play is consistent with constructivist learning theories, educators often include it into their curriculum. This method acknowledges that people build their knowledge by reflection and experience. This implies that during play, kids not only get a rush of excitement from the action but also pick up important life lessons about who they are and how the world works.

Reflective play also fosters creativity and problem-solving abilities. People develop their ability to think critically, make judgments, and adjust to changing conditions when they participate in open-ended activities. This feature is very helpful in preparing people for the obstacles they could encounter in many spheres of life.

Playing with reflection has advantages that go beyond young children. Reflective play may be beneficial for adults as well, offering a way for stress reduction, introspection, and enhanced mental health. Writing in a diary, creating art, or playing games with awareness may all be useful instruments for reflective play as adults.

To sum up, reflective play provides a comprehensive strategy for social and personal growth. Reflective play combines the components of self-expression, empathy, and critical thinking to create a potent tool that helps people of all ages manage their emotions, comprehend others, and develop the lifetime skills necessary for a happy and fulfilling existence.

When you first begin playing the guitar, consistency is essential.
The cornerstone of advancement on your guitar journey is consistency. The dedication to consistent practice becomes crucial while starting the journey to become proficient on this musical instrument. It takes consistent work to become proficient at playing the guitar, and the saying "consistency is key" couldn't fit this more well.

First and foremost, a strong foundation is established by constant practice. Frequent, concentrated practice improves finger dexterity and facilitates smoother chord changes by strengthening muscle memory. As you improve, this basic skill set serves as the basis for more complex approaches, which will enrich and enrich your musical journey.

Additionally, maintaining consistency helps one get a thorough grasp of fretboard navigation and music theory. Frequent practice helps you absorb chords, scales, and progressions, which improves your capacity for improvisation and free-form songwriting. When experimenting with new genres or improvising with other musicians, this intuitive understanding comes in quite handy.

Overcoming obstacles also heavily depends on consistency. It takes time to learn to play the guitar, and you will inevitably run across problems. But regular practice helps you approach challenges systematically, disassembling difficult methods into smaller, more manageable parts. This method cultivates perseverance and forbearance, two qualities that are crucial for mastering the guitar.

A regular practice schedule also develops discipline. A feeling of dedication and responsibility is ingrained when specific time is set up for guitar practice. This discipline has a good impact on various areas of your life in addition to music. Maintaining a routine becomes a transferable skill that improves your time management and overall efficiency.

Additionally, learning to play the guitar is a marathon rather than a sprint. Maintaining consistency aids in proper self-pacing, so averting fatigue and frustration. Long-term motivation and engagement are sustained via setting and achieving realistic objectives and persistently pursuing them.

To sum up, the key to success on your guitar journey is consistency. By committing to regular practice, you develop discipline, resilience, and a stronger bond with the instrument in addition to a solid technical basis. Thus, take up the guitar on a regular basis, remain dedicated, and allow consistency to be the secret to unlocking your creative potential.

Chapter 9

Finger independence

A key component of dexterity and fine motor control is finger independence. It describes how each finger may move independently of the others, enabling accurate and well-coordinated actions. This ability is essential for a variety of tasks, such as keyboarding and playing musical instruments.

Finger independence is crucial for creating complex melodies and unique notes in music, especially for piano and guitar performers. To increase their finger dexterity and coordination, musicians practice for hours on end. This raises their level of technical skill and adds to the performance's expressiveness.

When it comes to sports, finger independence is important for things like rock climbing and playing certain sports instruments like the clarinet or flute. Climbers need to be able to grip onto holds with only one finger, while wind instrument players need to be able to precisely press keys in order to generate certain tones.

One common everyday task where finger independence is sometimes taken for granted is typing on a keyboard. Each finger must press the appropriate key separately in order to type efficiently and accurately, which increases typing speed and lowers mistake rates. Strong finger independence allows typers to easily explore the keyboard.

Hand therapists commonly assist patients in regaining finger freedom after operations or injuries. Exercises for rehabilitation concentrate on strengthening and isolating each finger to promote faster healing and the restoration of functional hand motions.

Overall, finger independence is a talent that improves performance and usefulness in a variety of contexts, including the arts, sports, and daily duties. To acquire this skill, the complex connections between the brain and the muscles that govern each finger must be strengthened via specialized workouts and constant practice.

The Art of Practice and the Technical Conclusion

The foundation of mastery in the field of skill development and expertise is the combination of technical competency and the art of practice. The technical conclusion incorporates applied abilities and draws on the subtleties of real-world settings rather than being a simple summary of academic understanding.

A technical conclusion requires a thorough comprehension of underlying concepts, the development of sophisticated problem-solving skills, and the synthesis of solutions. This extends beyond the information found in textbooks and includes applying principles in real-world situations. Therefore, the technical conclusion denotes the skill of deftly navigating the complexities of a profession.

The art of practice—a purposeful and conscientious attempt to improve one's abilities via ongoing engagement—complements this technical proficiency. Practice is an intentional effort to improve skill, flexibility, and inventiveness rather than just doing things over and over again. It entails stepping beyond the box, accepting difficulties, and picking up lessons from both failure and achievement.

From science to the arts, there is a synergy between the technical result and the art of practice in many domains. In science, a thorough understanding of methodology and the repetitive nature of experimentation are essential for researchers to be able to derive significant conclusions from their work. Comparably, in the arts, a musician, painter, or writer's technical proficiency is honed with constant practice, resulting in the production of works that have depth and uniqueness.

Furthermore, practicing cultivates an attitude of continuous development, which promotes resiliency and persistence. Reaching a certain destination is not the sole goal; it's also about enjoying the process of improvement and development. In a world where change is inevitable and the capacity to adapt is highly valued, this way of thinking is essential.

In summary, the art of practice and the technical conclusion are interconnected components that help people become experts in their fields. Expertise is the result of a dynamic process that starts with embracing the technical components of a field and ends with continuously improving abilities via deliberate practice. The combination of technical expertise and skillful practice execution becomes essential as we negotiate the complexity of our chosen industries because it unlocks the greatest levels of competency and inventiveness.